SPORTS

DEANDRE HOPKINS

By Kevin Frederickson

Kaleidoscope

Minneapolis, MN

Your Front Row Seat to the Games

This edition is co-published by agreement between Kaleidoscope and World Book, Inc.

Kaleidoscope Publishing, Inc.
6012 Blue Circle Drive
Minnetonka, MN 55343 U.S.A.

World Book, Inc.
180 North LaSalle St., Suite 900
Chicago IL 60601 U.S.A.

Kaleidoscope ISBNs
978-1-64519-036-3 (library bound)
978-1-64494-193-5 (paperback)
978-1-64519-137-7 (ebook)

World Book ISBN
978-0-7166-4339-5 (library bound)

Library of Congress Control Number
2019940056

Printed in the United States of America.

TABLE OF CONTENTS

CHAPTER 1

Flying High

DeAndre Hopkins waits for the ball to be snapped. He's ready to run hard. The Houston Texans are taking on the New York Jets in Week 15 of the 2018 season. The game is in the second quarter, and the Texans lead 6–3.

The ball goes back to the quarterback. Hopkins dashes down the center of the field. A defender starts to run with him. Hopkins's eyes are straight ahead. He's looking right at the **end zone**. He's waiting for quarterback Deshaun Watson to throw him the ball.

FUN FACT
Hopkins had 421 of his 1,572 receiving yards in 2018 in the season's last three games.

DeAndre Hopkins dives to make a touchdown catch in a 2018 game with the New York Jets.

Hopkins fights for a touchdown grab later in the game, his eleventh of the season.

Moments later, Watson **launches** the ball down field. Hopkins looks up. He runs to the back of the end zone. He's trying to find the ball. The defender can't keep up with Hopkins.

The ball hangs in the air. It might be going over Hopkins's head. Hopkins leaps off the ground. He grabs the ball out of the air. The defender stands feet away from Hopkins. He's trying to figure out where the ball is. But Hopkins knows. He brings in the ball to his chest. He falls down. But he's in the end zone. Touchdown!

Later, the Texans fall behind. They trail in the fourth quarter. The score is 22–19. Watson drops back once again. Hopkins is running down the sideline. He's near the end zone. Watson sees Hopkins and throws a pass lightly into the air.

Hopkins sees the ball. But his hands are being held by a New York defender. Hopkins jumps into the air. His hands get free for a split second. He grabs the ball out of the air. The defender grabs him and brings him down. But Hopkins's feet land in the end zone. The ball is still in his hands. It's another touchdown. Houston goes on to win 29–22.

Hopkins dazzled fans with his catches. That made him a very popular player. With Hopkins, Houston had a chance in any game.

CAREER STATS

Through the 2018 season

GAMES PLAYED	95
RECEPTIONS	528
RECEIVING YARDS	7,437
TOUCHDOWNS	47
LONGEST CATCH (YARDS)	76

CHAPTER 2

A Star Is Born

DeAndre Hopkins faces the basket. He **dribbles** quickly. He has a **fierce** look on his face. He gets closer to the hoop. No defender can slow him down. DeAndre gets to the hoop. He leaps into the air. The ball is in his right hand. DeAndre throws it down through the hoop. The fans erupt.

His mom is in the stands. Sabrina Greenlee cheers on her son every chance she gets. But sometimes she can't make the games. She works more than one job. DeAndre's father passed away when he was five months old. DeAndre and his mom are very close. She works hard to pay all the family's bills.

DeAndre could soar through the air to dunk just like going up high for a catch.

DeAndre was born in Central, South Carolina, on June 6, 1992. He played football, basketball, and track & field growing up. He was good at all three sports. But his best sports were basketball and football.

FUN FACT
DeAndre played in seven games for Clemson's basketball team during the 2010–11 season.

He played both in college for the Clemson Tigers. DeAndre played just one year of basketball. But he shined on the football field. He had an amazing year in 2012. He caught 82 passes for 1,405 yards. He set a Clemson record with 18 touchdowns.

DeAndre was hard to catch in three seasons with the Clemson Tigers.

Where Hopkins Has Been

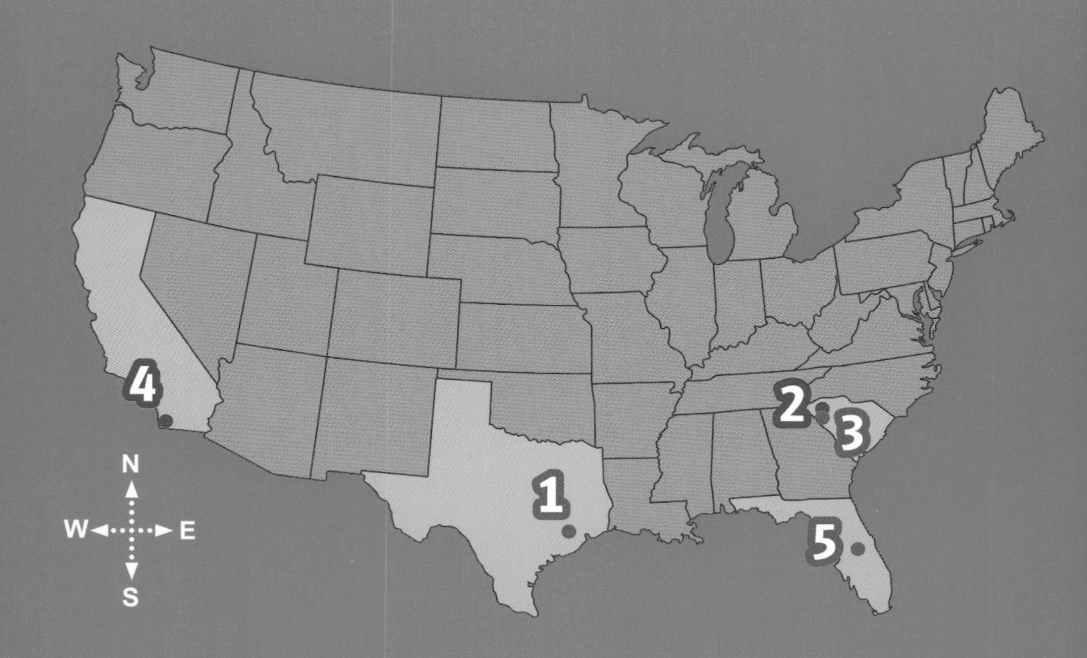

1 **Houston, Texas:** Where DeAndre Hopkins began his NFL career.

2 **Clemson, South Carolina:** Hopkins played three seasons here for the Tigers.

3 **Central, South Carolina:** Hopkins grew up and went to high school here.

4 **San Diego, California:** Hopkins played in his first NFL game here against the Chargers in 2013.

5 **Orlando, Florida:** Hopkins played in the Pro Bowl here in 2018 and 2019.

DeAndre was a star receiver at Clemson. He tied the school record with 27 career touchdowns. He was good enough to play in the pros. DeAndre left school a year early to try to play in the National Football League (NFL).

The Houston Texans chose DeAndre in the first round of the 2013 NFL Draft. He was the first receiver they had taken in the first round since 2003. That earlier player was Andre Johnson. He became the best receiver in Texans history. The team thought DeAndre could be just as good.

DeAndre catches a pass in his first NFL training camp with the Texans.

CHAPTER 3

Giving Back

DeAndre Hopkins left his hometown after high school. But he never forgot about it. He returns often to give back. He walks into an elementary school. He carries backpacks filled with pencils, folders, and markers. A young child runs toward him. He puts a book bag on the kid's shoulders. The kid has a smile that goes from ear to ear.

At lunch time, students run to the cafeteria. They see the normal cafeteria workers. Then they see Hopkins. He holds a blue tray in his hand. A student approaches. Hopkins hands the student a tray full of meat and veggies. Hopkins loves meeting kids. They look up to him.

Hopkins signs autographs for fans while playing in a charity softball game in Houston.

Hopkins leaps into the crowd to celebrate a touchdown in 2014.

Hopkins spends his time away from football helping people. He runs an **organization** called S.M.O.O.O.T.H. Inc. It helps women and children. His mom helps out a lot with the **charity**. She works with women who have been hit by their partners.

HONORING JAZMINE

Hopkins was getting ready for a playoff game in 2018. Then he saw some bad news. A girl in Houston was shot earlier that week. Her name was Jazmine Barnes. She was only seven years old. Hopkins wanted to help. He decided to donate part of his paycheck for that game to Jazmine's family. He sent $29,000 to help pay for her funeral.

Back in Houston, Hopkins is not alone. His sister, Kesha Smith, lives there. They can talk about life and football. Both play wide receiver. Kesha plays for the Houston Wildcats. They are a women's football team. She is also a basketball trainer.

Even Hopkins's nickname reminds him of family. He is known as Nuk. The name came from his mom. Nuk is a brand of pacifier. It was the only kind Hopkins liked as a baby. So the name stuck. Now, even his teammates call him Nuk.

FUN FACT

Hopkins has played in NRG Stadium since entering the league. The Texans have used the stadium since the team formed in 2002.

Hopkins hands the ball to a fan after scoring a touchdown in 2017.

CHAPTER 4

Hopkins tries to make a one-handed catch in his NFL debut in 2013.

The Next Step

DeAndre Hopkins ran down the sideline. A Tennessee Titans defender followed him each step of the way. Hopkins raised his hand high in the air. He wanted quarterback Matt Schaub to throw him a pass. The ball soared through the air. Hopkins went up for it. Two Titans went up with him. Hopkins grabbed it out of the air.

Hopkins was playing in his second NFL game in 2013. He already had the confidence to call for the ball. He knew what he could do on the field. Everyone else was about to find out, too.

Hopkins celebrates with teammate Demaryius Thomas after a touchdown catch.

Two plays later, Schaub dropped back three steps. He looked to the right. Hopkins ran into the end zone. A defender was right with him. But Schaub trusted Hopkins. He threw it anyway. Hopkins went up for it. He nabbed it out of the air. Touchdown! It was Hopkins's first touchdown in the NFL. And it gave Houston the win.

The Texans tried several different quarterbacks. Hopkins had success with all of them. He made his first Pro Bowl after the 2015 season. But a new teammate helped him reach new heights.

Hopkins throws out the first pitch at a Houston Astros baseball game.

CAREER TIMELINE

1992

June 6, 1992
DeAndre Hopkins is born in Central, South Carolina.

2010

September 4, 2010
Hopkins plays his first college football game with Clemson.

2013

2013
Hopkins decides to leave school and go to the NFL.

2013

April 25, 2013
Hopkins is drafted by the Houston Texas in the first round.

2013

September 15, 2013
Hopkins catches his first NFL touchdown pass, and the Texans win the game.

2016

January 9, 2016
Hopkins plays in his first playoff game.

2016

January 31, 2016
Hopkins plays in his first Pro Bowl.

The Texans drafted quarterback Deshaun Watson in 2017. He also had played at Clemson. He and Hopkins never played together. But Hopkins watched his games. They became fast friends.

Hopkins caught Watson's first career touchdown pass in 2017. Watson faked a handoff. He looked for Hopkins.

Watson and Hopkins have formed a dynamic duo for the Texans.

He threw over the middle. Touchdown! But the Texans lost the game. Watson got better. It helped to have a star like Hopkins on his team.

Hopkins also got better with Watson on board. He set a career high for catches and yards in 2018. The future is bright for Hopkins and the Texans.

BEYOND THE BOOK

After reading the book, it's time to think about what you learned. Try the following exercises to jumpstart your ideas.

THINK

DIFFERENT SOURCES. What type of sources could you use to find out more about DeAndre Hopkins's college career? How could each source be useful?

CREATE

PRIMARY SOURCES. Primary sources are documents or sources that were made at the time of an event. They might include interviews, photos, and videos. Create a list of primary sources that talk about DeAndre Hopkins. What kinds of information could you learn from these sources?

SHARE

WHAT'S YOUR OPINION? In Chapter Four, it says that Hopkins's career was helped by Houston bringing in Deshaun Watson. Do you agree with that opinion? Provide evidence for or against it. Then, share your opinion with a friend. Does the friend find the argument convincing?

GROW

REAL LIFE RESEARCH. What kind of place could you go to learn more about football and DeAndre Hopkins? What are some other things you could learn by visiting this place?

Visit *www.ninjaresearcher.com/0363* to learn how to take your research skills and book report writing to the next level!

DIGITAL LITERACY TOOLS

SEARCH LIKE A PRO

Learn about how to use search engines to find useful websites.

FACT OR FAKE?

Discover how you can tell a trusted website from an untrustworthy resource.

TEXT DETECTIVE

Explore how to zero in on the information you need most.

SHOW YOUR WORK

Research responsibly—learn how to cite sources.

WRITE

GET TO THE POINT

Learn how to express your main ideas.

PLAN OF ATTACK

Learn prewriting exercises and create an outline.

DOWNLOADABLE REPORT FORMS

Further Resources

BOOKS

Adamson, Thomas K. *The Houston Texans Story*. Bellwether, 2017.

Morey, Allan. *Superstars of the Houston Texans*. Amicus, 2019.

Norman, J. T. *Houston Texans*. Abdo Publishing, 2017.

WEBSITES

FACTSURFER

Factsurfer.com gives you a safe, fun way to find more information.

1. Go to www.factsurfer.com.
2. Enter "DeAndre Hopkins" into the search box and click .
3. Select your book cover to see a list of related websites.

Glossary

charity: A charity is a group that helps people in need. Hopkins runs a charity that helps women and children.

dribble: To dribble means to bounce the basketball off the floor. Hopkins dribbles the ball to the hoop before dunking the ball.

end zone: The end zone is where someone has to go to score a touchdown. Hopkins caught the pass and ran into the end zone for a touchdown.

fierce: Something is fierce when it is very aggressive. Hopkins had a fierce look on his face when he tried to catch a touchdown pass.

launch: Something is launched when it is thrown with a lot of force. The quarterback launched a pass far down the field to Hopkins.

organization: An organization is a group of people with a particular goal. Hopkins is part of the Houston Texans organization.

Index

PHOTO CREDITS

The images in this book are reproduced through the courtesy of: Winslow Townson/Panini/AP Images, front cover (center); Kevin Terrell/AP Images, front cover (right); Margaret Bowles/AP Images, p. 3; dean bertoncelj/Shutterstock Images, p. 4; Adam Hunger/AP Images, pp. 4–5, 6–7; Jeff Bukowski/Shutterstock Images, pp. 8, 25 (helmet); Red Line Editorial, pp. 9 (chart), 14, 25 (chart); Greg Trott/AP Images, p. 9 (DeAndre Hopkins); Michelle Donahue Hillison/Shutterstock Images, pp. 10–11; Jamie Lamor Thompson/Shutterstock Images, pp. 12, 25 (flag); Patrick Collard/AP Images, pp. 12–13; Pat Sullivan/AP Images, p. 15; Matt Patterson/AP Images, pp. 16–17, 18–19; Katherine Welles/Shutterstock Images, p. 20; David J. Phillip/AP Images, pp. 21, 26–27; Gregory Bull/AP Images, p. 22; Bill Kostroun/AP Images, p. 23; Bob Levey/AP Images, p. 24; CE Photography/Shutterstock Images, p. 30.

ABOUT THE AUTHOR

Kevin Frederickson is a writer who lives with his goldendoodle in Cincinnati, Ohio. He has written other children's books throughout his decade-long career in the publishing industry.